Table of Contents

I0664642

The Journey of Akbar

Library of Congress Control Number: 2025905931

Dedicated to:

my parents

George A. Wallace
Irene Edna Wallace

my son

Kadeem M. Wallace

&

The Bennett and Wallace Family

The Jeffers, Woods, and Herbert Family

"my love is eternal"

INTRODUCTION

This anthology of poems bear witness to a journey and the power of survival. They capture the soul of everyday realities. They travel the scope of the complications of our faith, our families, our friendships, life, love, loss, dreams, and our aspirations, all set against the environment of an island's life experience coupled with the familiarities of living in New York City. From soaring buildings to the hidden alleyways of the "El Campo," each poem offers a valid view of life's circumstances and experiences. Taking us to journeys of where we were, where we are, and where we will be. As you read through these pages, I hope you find inspiration, connection, and a deeper appreciation for the rich and varied stories that shape our lives.

Songs from The Trenches

Song 1: In Edna's voice

"Momma did say
There will be times like these
Momma did say
Son, you have to hold on to your dreams
Momma did say
Life is full of choices
Momma did say son, you got to believe"

Song 2: As simple as wallpaper

"I built my house of stone
Because I wanted to be on my own
She built her house of sticks
Could not have pictured this
Love came in and took over our souls
And now we live in a house of love, painted in gold"

Song 3: Win in colors

"In the poverty there is wisdom
You win and win, then lose some
But life is like a colored circle
Shaded in blue, green, and purple
So pick your color of the day
You would be a winner anyway"

"they say when you take an early morning walk you gain an eagle's view into your soul"

The Oracle of Her

It was early Sunday morning
I was still in bed
I was unsure if I was dreaming
My thoughts walked in and began to take control
It took me from Pelham Gardens to Prickley Pear
Then unto an airborne journey into this new world
I am gliding, the spaceship kept on ascending
The voyage made me feel so good
Took me to heights of reasons that I once misunderstood
All my regrets and sorrows began to appear
Then poof! Look how soon they disappear
An angelic light from over yonder came into my zone
At that ripe moment I knew I was not alone
I could hear a soft voice singing
Singing one of those negro spirituals, it was ever so clear
I looked around me
Contentment was everywhere
And to my surprise, Irene Edna Wallace, my mother,
She was smiling, with welcoming arms, just standing there

The Birth of You

"Masha Allah"
You were born in the middle of a snow storm
Under a February's dull and weakened sun
We used blankets, faith, and love, to keep you warm
Our anxiety and expectations had just begun
Yet, there we stood for hours, in jubilance, looking over you
Asking the heavens for guidance, and to see us through
And when you stirred, or smiled, or cried?
Our feelings, in those moments, were of our love for you

Love of Sisters

O ye daughters of my mother, and sisters of mine
I have loved you then, as now
And shall love you all down through infinity
In the countless hours we have spent together in conversations
Talking about life's challenges and stuff
But time, times time, is never enough
Never will my love for you waiver
It is etched in ageless stones
Just Like those that keeps the great pyramids standing tall and strong
in the sands of our motherland
You are blossoms in the winter snow
Roses in the horrid desert sand
Refuge from a raging storm
You bring tears to my eyes
Joyful tears of such good memories
In our great journey from birth to death
I stand to ask, when have I loved you less?
I shall honor you today, and beyond tomorrow
May it be joys of laughter, or pains of sorrow
I shall do what our ancestors asked of me
I shall love you beyond the miles mine eyes can see
Then proudly! I shall love you all down through eternity

Soul Cry

Sorrow and pain sits next me
Joy and laughter dwindled into a distant memory
I live life in the darkness
Sunlight no longer has meaning or comes inside to kiss on me
So I cried, how could this be?
The loss of my mother, I cried, it was so painful
I asked the heavens to open up and let me in
The pain feels like I am fighting a losing battle
In a war I cannot win
My soul cries

It is a new day, I am up early
I could feel the coming energy
The morning sun brings out the fight in me
Even though I am down, I am not out
"It is time for you to step up and win"
That's what a voice in the distance stood to say
Ready to face whatever this sadness brings
For now, I know, I could win this thing
Joy and laughter began resurfacing, I am winning
My soul cries

There stood this new beginning
And there is this renewed happiness deep within
My tears dries, I am now smiling
Slowly, but surely, happiness comes in to do her thing
Joy takes over in everything, yep! I am winning

A Conversation with Grandma

She said, "Son, look around you what do you see
Is it my age? for this should never be"
In my life's journey I have learnt how to live with change
You know, "roll with the punches," having things rearranged
But folks have taken it further, and started to spill a rage
The measurement of civility no longer has a gauge
As if society thinking's came in from out-of-space
The followers are leading, and the leaders are following
Malice got brazen and showed her stubborn face
Where are we going? What is going on?
Seems like listening and dialogue are all gone
The role of the genders are being reversed
As technologies gets better, our scruples gets worst
Life's sweet melons have lost their taste
I am so disappointed, I am tired, oh what a waste
By tomorrow, believe me!
I'll ask the heavens to take me away from this place

The Color of Me

This is who I am, I am of you
I bear all of your qualities
From my head down to my very toes
My ancestors came out of Alkebulan, and that's a fact
I am black!
I am not like some of the others, who would quickly tell you that they
are half this or quarter that
They failed to understand the power of their heritage
Cowards I say, or just ill-informed rootless brats
Nationalities and country's flags are just walls
Placed there to make me feel that I am not connected to you
They try so hard to weaken your potent brew
But you are embedded in my very soul, and everything that is true
about me
 O Motherland!, O Alkebulan! Please forgive them
Those who have tried their hardest to distance themselves from you
For the miles they have traveled and the successes they have gained
Takes them to journeys and right back to you again
The apple and the apple's tree are parts of a cycle
Our journey, our history, would have it no other way
There she stood between yesterday and tomorrow
All down through faith, family, happiness, and sorrows
She is asking, "come home"
Not necessarily in the physical but in the mental
Come home! Come on home o ye children! She awaits you
She has never denied you, and for that you should be grateful

The Journey of Akbar

As-Salaam Alaikum
Sometimes the pain and sorrow come in a lump sum
You win, you lose some, Life is crazy
His father died when he was just a baby
His struggle is real
His life went south, unwillingly, really quickly
His mother tried her best to keep a roof over his head
Voices in the distance told her
Honey child don't you surrender
Don't you put your hands out and begin to beg
She saw her life's journey flash before her
While looking up at the ceiling
She prefers to fight standing up
Then seek a truce by crying and kneeling
She knows every turn in life has meaning
She got up and walked outside to look at the sky
She stood there wondering, asking the reasons why
She tries
For she was determined not to let time and purpose pass her by
Or go sit in a corner, be a loser, complain and cry
So, she asked for divine guidance

She stormed the weather
The sorrow and pain pushed her to do better
Her struggle stood there
But she would not surrender
Across the way, there goes her baby boy playing in the street
She could hear his old puma sneakers losing to the hot concrete
Later that night
He fights like hell to fall asleep
He is still hungry

But never complained about the little he had to eat
He knows that there is wisdom in the poverty
He could hear his mother crying at the kitchen table
While sipping on a cup of Oolong tea
He whispered, "cry for them mother,"
"Please don't you cry for me"
He knew a better tomorrow was on its' way
After reading a surah from the Quran, he planned his day
Ready to face these demons, comes what may
Then he asked for divine guidance

Good Over Evil

Please save my soul today
From the fools who came in to scorn
But they failed, so they packed up and ran away
They now wished they were never born
All their good times and riches all gone
That is why I am here kneeling to pray
Please lend them another waiting day
Let them see the light and seek what's right
For all birds are not blessed with the power of flight
There is no new day without the darkness of night

Please save my soul today
Look at the greatness you have brought to me
Allowing me to forgive
And rise above the worst that they wish for me
The evil that they sold up in here
Has flown outside and thawed into the atmosphere
That is why I am here kneeling to ask
Please give those weak souls another chance
Let them see the light and do what's right
For all birds are not blessed with the power of flight

Please save my soul today
If love is true, it could never walk away
We surrendered our souls to prayer
Here comes tomorrow forget the heathens of the day
For all birds are not blessed with the power of flight
Be better, speak truth, walk your journey into the light

Union Strong

Joseph Joey DiCaprio from Brooklyn

Was a proud union man

A scab was not a person he respected,

But he will still lend him a helping hand

He worked thirty-five long years

He was always on the grind

But found time to coach his son's softball team

And walked a picket line

From bachelor-life to his own family

From journeyman, to shoppy, to retiree

Today we got the sad news that Joey had lost his fight

And at his wake someone stood to say, "the union was his life"

Existing In My Mind

What if I was never born
I probably be a shooting star, glittering or sparkling, on and on

What if I was rocketed in from out of space
I will perhaps be neutral, having no nationality, creed or race

What if I could never love or hate
War and peace would probably find ways to cooperate

What if I have never experienced happiness or sorrow
I probably be lost or forgotten by yesterday, or by tomorrow

What if I could never idle or dance
Life's sweet music would have lost its chance

What if I could never laugh or cry
I probably be robotic, synthetic or living a lie

...And when it is all said and done
   Would all these circumstances bring my salvation?

A Note From The Frontline

They ditched him in a bottomless pit
And left him there to die
And just like Joseph he suffered
But faith had him survived
Don't you ever let obstacles ruin your day
They would always come in
but it's on you to have them come for vacation and then decide to
stay
Great lessons he had learnt
And great experiences he had gained
Prayer and laughter always drowns out the evil in them
For sufferings runs from pain
He counted his blessings everyday
As Grandpa Bennett always said, tomorrow brings a better day
Open up the gates and let the troupes through
For your only hurdle or stumbling block is you
The clouds came in, then it rained,
followed by the hotness of the sun
The soldier kneeled in tears, full of puzzlement
When he realized his conflict never required a gun

We Rise Above the Circumstances

These are the forgotten people
Some of them live in those NYCHA housings
Each new day they suffer
She said, "they say our lives lack meaning"
So they cast their eyes, and look down on us
As if our lives have no purpose
Just like the people of Irish Town, Flint, Soweto,
Palenque, Ramallah, Riga, Handsworth, Morrisania
And all the other hood-strong places
We live where life is the hardest, but we survive
Wisdom, untapped talent, and courage
Breathes down here in the poverty
So we walked through these unjust alleyways "continually"
Circumstances of life has put us here
And so, we fight to leave these cages year after year
Verily, verily
Our lives do have meaning
Through it all we keep it strong
We stay vigilant for opportunities, if they shall come along
Life situations came in to throw stones at us
We fight! We won!
For our lives do have purpose

Regrets

Thomas "Glitzy" McKenzie, stands gazing out into the ocean
He stood there, on the edge of a dock
He looks into the heavens praying
Then slowly look at a floating party on a passing adorned yacht
He looks down at his shining Stefano Ricci's
Then he peeps at his Rolex watch
He looks so withdrawn, so deserted,
As if he were a writer experiencing a writer's block
He thinks of his successes, his possessions
All the "baddies" he has had
He is standing there, looking miserable, dumbfounded, and sad
All his life he was told, work hard, play hard, "make all that money man," get rich! reap all its' rewards
He had no time to develop real relationships, or find true love
And all his "baddies" were fakes and frauds
This brings us to the reason why he is there standing on the dock
He just came from his doctor, his blood-work results threw him into a panic, for he felt his wellbeing was as solid as a rock
He now recognizes he no longer needs, the extra trimmings, the flashy threads, the Rolex watch
Sadly, he found out he is slowly dying
He feels that his fleeting time would be hastened, if measured by a timetable clock
He now see all of his possessions as a "fugazzi," a heavy burden, pointless, unusable, a dead stock

Inside His Thoughts

He is jazzy, really cunning
He is a smooth talker, a new yorker
He said, he is so rich and healthy
He'll probably live forever
Now that he is older, he is so stuck in his ways
He refuses to date those "lunchables,"
"The level-ups," and women around his age
He learnt early that a zebra never loses it stripes
So he stayed far away as possible from
 "the loud mouths," "the neck-rollers" and "the hallelujah" types
Then they would want you to believe
He is crazy, he is unrealistic, he is finished, he is living a lie
Remember! This is his life folks, his choices
If you have issues? You need not apply
They say he is arrogant, or he is going through a phase
For he only chooses, those "baddies"
that are forever cat-walking on stage
Last week in conversation
With his resentful, unhappy, lying-ass ex-wife
She said, "if given the option,
She will cut-off his tail with a carving knife"
But the one thing my life has taught me is that
"I do not need a man"
The last time we saw her...
She was joyriding with two well-groomed Yokies
She was bitter, very bitter, dressed sleezy
She was driving a Tesla van

House of Pain

If there is nothing to lose
Then there is nothing to gain
Sunshine would not mean a thing
if she does not welcome in the clouds of rain
Then why fight this battle if the victory would be in vain
There will be no joy in this journey
If nothing was attained
The beautiful garden outside blooms, but brings no joy
In this house of pain

We have so much work to do
"Long road ahead" so face the day
That is what the oracle came in to say
Avenues of life to pursue
Looking into the heavens seeking a clue
Here comes those clouds of rain
Then why fight this continuous battle
If the victory would be in vain
Yes! Tell them I said it
And I will say it again
The beautiful garden outside blooms, but brings no joy
In this house of pain

Then Comes The Vacation Blues

There is something in the air
That is the reason I picked this season
I made my intentions noticeably clear
Pristine weather, sunshine, and a love affair
Cool night, dim lights, decent food, and locally made "moonshine"
All that big city life living, gets left behind
An island breeze, coconut trees, serenity everywhere
Laughter, slow dancing, insightful conversations, and romance
Selflessly, she took me there
In that moment I found my peace
It is like swimming in the seawater
Out there on Cockleshell Bay Beach
Or sitting around with the locals, politicking
In the sea breezed Village of Keys
Soon after, we are reasoning with a "Rasta" brother
Way into the stillness of the eve
Eating stew fish and coconut dumplings
While smoking on home grown leaves
It is there I realized vacations are never slow
This is one for the pages, pack it up "honey dip,"
Sadly, we leave this peacefulness tomorrow

Yesterday Sends Tomorrow

Thanksgiving Day I dined with family
I sat there in happiness, reunited with a childhood friend
Our bond and trust grew out of authenticity
So, there was no leeway for false pretense
The missing years went on by so quickly
We face life's challenges, they come with ups and downs
We shall not live our lives of "buts and maybes"
We keep it one hundred, our alliance was always sound
Situation after situation we had missed year after year
She said, bro, we should count our blessings, be thankful
We should say a prayer for we are still here
In the story of our absence, and our devotion
We had no pages or chapters to amend
Faith has such celestial energies
That's why it is heavenly sent
Real friendships, they last forever
That's why infinity has no end

To find the Silence

'Buscando calma' I whispered
As I made a mental toast
I sat at the hilltop spellbound
Overlooking the island's coast
This is where the Atlantic Ocean kisses the Carib's Sea
There I experienced true silence
No cars or people, just me
Birds flew by to journeys unknown
That takes them to places so far away from home
The sun is in its glory but cannot do a thing
To my dark and shiny Bantu skin
I too shall fly to a distance shore fulfilling a dream
For destiny and courage are players on life's team
But one thing that shall remain continuously
Sitting watching out at the ocean, for It comforts me

Ocean of Love

Wherever I shall be
My love for you will never abundant me
All my emotions are guided by beaches, seas and oceans
All their moods, tides, and waves
Determines how I live my life
How I love, my happiness and how I should behave
I sat in silence observing and worshiping her for hours
I embraced all her majestic powers
Every day she teaches me something new
Which brings me forever closer to you
One daring, humid, sunny, summer afternoon
I swam and swam
Until I forgot where I was, and who I am
I kept on swimming
Yet I could not understand
Why she kept on pushing me
Pushing me back to land

The What if's

What if my best days are already gone
Oh well! that's sucks!
But I will still have to carry on
What if my family walks away
I will complain and cry but love them anyway
Then denounce their reasons everyday
What if my woman claims she does not love me anymore
I will be saddened, then probably in anger call her a three-O-four
Hurriedly, but graciously walk her to the door
What if the pagans try to ruin my life
I will laugh it off because' I will still survive
What if, what ifs came with what if's
I will be pissed, and in frustration I will set it off
Perhaps get crazy like Chris Rock and "willing" Smith
"Run amok! you know! flip the script
Bite my pinkie, throw a fit
Maybe pull that "burner" up off my hip
Frankly, Skip?
I am so thankful these are all 'what if's

Sounds of Music

They say when you only dance to music
It could take you away from your reality
I would rather sit and listen to music
For her rhythms endures the fight in me
My ancestors, yes! they danced, mostly for ritual reasons
Good crops, new births, great harvest
Bountifulness in all its' seasons
If I only dance to music
What good would it do or bring to me?
I would rather sit and listen to music
For it keeps me mindful of my reality
That sweet, deep, melodic music
It brings me to a place of tranquility
Then...
She pours that added ingredient, which is needed for my creativity

The Rage of The Day

It's a new day
For the sun just came out
The streets are all crowded, people shopping all about
There is a man on the run, Yo Naj! he has a gun
And his aim is to aid his convictions
He is fed up, put his street cred up, it's a set up
But does he care?
It's too much to bear
that's when he discharged gunfire everywhere
He feels like he is losing everything
His failures are mounting, his reign is dwindling
He feels like he is out here on his own
And this country, this America, belongs to him
He buys into that right-wing rhetoric
The pressure of losing "his country" falls on him like a brick
His cellphone he continuously swipes, day and night
Got caught up in the "us" versus "them" and the deep state hype
Then, so many communities he began to dislike
And like a true Nazi, a bigot, a racist, he holds no shame
He stood up like "Il Duce" and relished the fame
That's when a sniper on the rooftop took aim

The Closeness of Horror

Logan McNair lived in the attic
At the corner house on Fielding Street
We saw him going off to work, dressed nicely
Early every morning, six days a week
He always gave a greeting to everyone he saw
We all were astonished and confused
When the blue shirts rushed in to enforce the law
This can't be happening, what did he do?
Lies, these are just rumors, and they are untrue
The one day he did not work
He spent it volunteering, then he went off to church
We came to find out that these shenanigans were all rehearsed
Then the "bochinche" got even worst
He was accused of a rape and a robbery near Universe
They found lots of female clothing
A Sephora make up kit, Fenty products, and a Gucci purse
Fentanyl paraphernalia, then they found him comatose
One month later, while out on bond, "shh! lean in, come in close"
"They found him in the attic, dress like the Riddler"
"He died of an overdose"

I Will Find You

Even though it has been years since you have been gone
It was difficult at first, but I carried on
Parts of me still wished you were here
Thoughts of you lingered year after year
A "connect" told me she once saw you, at Bunker Hill Monument just
sitting there
Reality has taken us to different paths
A journey that left us broken hearted
It was agonizing, for this love, our love, was real
Still missing you, still care
But If faith is true
I still believe
That one day, my regrets shall find you

A Prayer for the Daybreak

You are my rock and my creator
In my everyday struggles there are lessons learnt
Humility brings incite
You have never left me alone
When evil comes to inflict harm
You have guided me down a protective path
I wish no one failure, for success produces the highest energy
Surround me always with the kindest of people
For love could never be defeated
Let my mistakes and my shortcomings be known
For imperfections keeps me trying to do better
In my darkest hour
you shine light on my tomorrow
By bringing me love over hate
And joy over sorrow
I am proud of who I am
I am a son, a brother, an uncle, a father and a friend
I feel rewarded for my Alkebulan heritage
For Alkebulan has given so much to humanity
To my mother and her mother, and her mother's mother
To my father and his father, and his father's father
These ancestors have prayed for my salvation, and your continuous
blessing and guidance over me
O Allah, remember me always
Yesterday, today, and tomorrow
Bismillah!!

High Society

He sat there with his dog in the park across the way
Watching where the rich folks live
He watches them enter the park to walk their dogs and socialize with
each other
He mingles with the other dog owners and have small conversations
about dogs, the best restaurants, and the day's weather
For an hour or two, he forgets about his tomorrow
Quickly he begins to feel at home
What stocks did your broker buy you today?
Are you folks going to The Hamptons for the holiday?
What a way to live
These are some of the questions asked amongst the privileged

However, ...
They are unaware of his pain, his struggle,
His frustration and his budgeted living
For them he is just another rich dude walking his dog
He sips on a cup of cheap coffee he had just bought
It is just another day for him, living near Central Park North

The Return of Love

In the distance, I could hear her cry
I felt her pain and sorrow
But don't you worry *Neema Jones*
They will all disappear by tomorrow
He is the one man she has ever loved
What was he thinking of?
He has run off to seek a future of fame
He should have been ashamed, was it all a game?
She cried, she cried

Now that I am standing next to her
I could see a glimpse of a smile
Here come her clouds of laughter
For she knew her calamity was only for awhile
He was the one man she had ever loved
What was he thinking of?
He ran off to seek prosperity of fame
Seem like it was all in vain, for nothing was attained
She smiled, she smiled,
As a familiar voice in the distance called out her name

Tell The Truth

Am I the only one that cries?
When people come with tales of lies
Please open your souls, ears and eyes
To realize,
That truth is rewarded beyond money, or family ties
So, tell the truth

They say when a newborn baby cry
It is celestial messages beaming from the sky
They pour in like bees, or swarms of flies
To realize,
The search for truth makes the phoenix rise
So, tell the truth

In life's journey we face lows and highs
We win when we fly above the clouds of lies
Truth would never live a life disguised
To realize,
Eventually she picks the moment to vaporize your lies
So, tell the truth

The Ethos

The pulse of the culture
Is in the hearts and souls of the dark-skin people
It is in their speech, their music, their swagger
It is in their food, their mood, it is their attitude
There you go marginalizing them
Knowing full well that they are the fruits of the culture
Look around you!
Talent and wisdom comes out of the poverty
In your town, in your province, in your city
The heavens know that's true, so why not you?
They know that they are the forgotten people
Living down there where life is the hardest
You feel so strong to say they are weak
To acquire your profits, it's their energies you seek
Here comes your hypocrisy in your everyday speech
Asking...why don't they pick themselves up off the ground?
Answer...if a tree falls in the forest, does it make a sound?
They say those who win, they would never compromise
But we all need each other to prosper, to survive
I am sure we all seek "better" for our daily lives
So, they fight, the fight, to survive

A Traveler's Wish

One sleep-in morning
While lying in bed with my girl
I whispered in her ears softly
Let's get dressed and see the world!
Let's go see the continents, the seas,
the lakes, the rivers, and the oceans
The plains, the valleys, the mountains
All samples of God's creation
Then let us pause for a minute to pray for earth's people
Those in the struggle, with struggle credentials, suffering
Living out their situations

Let's travel by cars, trains, ships and planes
Let us visit kingdoms, towns and villages
Out of where our ancestors came
There we will enjoy fresh fruits, fresh fish
Drinks made from happiness, love and sugarcane
We will hold hands while walking down the unpaved walkways
That leads to Redemption Lane
We will stand in the horrid summer sun
Awaiting the rewarding showers of rain
Then let's promise each other
We will never lose focus or purpose in our lives ever again

Standing For Something

Babygirl, image is everything
How could you be taken seriously
Having all those foreign markings, inked in your skin
Forever wanting more, for wearing less
I am not impressed
You wear all those dreadful bonnets and fake images of hair
Clowning the culture, I am pissed, so pissed
Woman I am leaving, for you made your values clear
With all that hood-bait you bring up in here
Your choices are losing, from whence they begun
An inner voice keeps telling me, this is crazy, so run forest run
I will rather stand tall to get beat down, for my knees are weak
Plus kneeling to pray is the only time my knees hit the ground
The problem is real, we need a solution

Brother man, image is everything
How could she stand tall next to you
When you don't stand for anything
Each day your persona becomes more and more feminine
We all know what that would bring
How do you want to be remembered?
Out here in these streets of confusion
Which begs the question
Who is following? Who is leading?
The situation is slick and it's not leaving
Are you going to stand up and fight to win?
Or sit it out, and wish for an acceptable ending?
Are you going to stand up and lead the fight?
Fight like a soldier all through the night
brother man, brother man
Explain it to me, cousin
Make me understand

Night & Day

I want to sail the endless sea
Where only the wind
The sun, and the heavens, could find me
I want to sail the ocean so far away
That day is night and night is day
When the untamed tides swells
Sailing make me feel so free
That sorrow and regrets are light years behind me
When the sun hides her face
Her sister the moon steps in to take her place
Everything flows so true
So pure, so right
That night is day
And day is night

To Ride With Her

She's so beautiful, a good listener
Her smile brings the fire
She took me from highways of kindness
To parkways then streets of desire
She is loyal, for a deceiving chick she could never be
Didn't say she is perfect, but she is exactly what I want for me
She gets my jokes, she laughs then pokes
She strives to be better, a real "go-getter"
And that's why I am riding with her

She is calm and soft, she is a natural beauty
She lives for duty, "God damn that booty"
Her eyes are hypnotic, so bright and clear
No bonnets, no inks, no wigs or weaves
I love it when she braids her hair
She puts in work, she shuns the pork
She storms the weather, she loves the summer
And that's why I am riding with her

She is caring, she is God fearing
Daring, forever sharing
She is as humble as can be
Didn't say she is perfect, but she is the right gal for me
She brings a new chapter, she is the "it" factor
And that's why I am riding with her

A King's Life

An old man sits reminiscing
Reflecting on his life, his children, his rise and fall
Telling himself that if there wasn't for bad luck
He'll have no luck at all
He speaks of his journey
A journey with so many twists and turns
The many women he had bamboozled
The bridges he had burnt
Then he met this worthy woman, whom he married
He loved her with his heart and soul
But she fed him well-prepared fibbed lunches
And she was never bronze, silver or gold
Try not to convince him otherwise, for he lives in a delusional world
He sits daily on a park's bench airing out his soul
He still eats like a king
But he live life with his unhappiness
In a world that is crumbling

Powder Pyramid

I am living better now
Government is trying to figure out how
I have extra bitcoins and paper money
A mocha skin chick I call her sunny
A mansion up on the hill
A couple of acres down in "Bennettville"
A side-chick Stashed away
She will never have a wedding day
A boss-chick called Sue
We shared a love nest over on Burke Avenue
A pound of high-grade woo
A vain and boastful cockatoo
A pacific time-sharing pad
A stash-house fortified up on Amsterdam
Stacks in an offshore bank
I'm rich bitch! And I have you to thank

I Got Lucky

In my garden there stood this kindhearted rose
Who knew I would be blessed with one of those?
She wanted to hear my life story
My thoughts, and dreams
my highs and lows, my in between
Opportunity that I had missed
My years of pimping, yeah! I had found my niche
I could not have pictured this
But then here came the switch
We clicked; we went on several dates
Oh no! for none of them were great!
Perfect! is what comes to mind
And this kept on recurring every time
I got lucky

The Riff Raffs

They came with crock pots, d m's, and podcasts
With stock holdings in Apple, Meta, and Comcast
Tablets and I-phones, rainbow-colored cooking pans
Passive Incomes, A I, Facebook, Tiktok and Instagram
Online food shopping, Twitter, and Uber vans
With Tattoos on their necks and hands
They have conversations embedded in abbreviations
Multicultural family life and everyday liberal-minded situations
Group chats depicted in slang
They party with bottles on bottles of Cîroc
Vegan foods, Amapiano and Rap music
In the distance you could hear it
Family and friends coupled with laughter
Prayer and worship the morning after
An occasional smell of weed
They claim it gives them time to breathe, and heal from the woes of
yesterday
Even thou the other neighbors look down on them
I must say they seems so happy, loving and contented
Full of life's promises, living life, they are very energized
They all want to prosper
I could not help but invite myself over
So, I devised a plan

Friendships

I do not have a lot of them
But the lasting ones comes from way back when
Of course I have had friendships on my journey
I meet new people everyday
But just like mountains behind in the distance
With our journey, they will ultimately wane away
The difficulties and the rewards, the in-between
In those trenches, we fought together
But still took time out to clutch a dream
My friendship which I am of just a half
Go ask about me
They will tell you
I have always made it easier
For us to sit around and laugh!

Yesterday's bonds

Yo bro,
We formed these eternal bonds way back then
From Market Street to Seaton Street
Forever you are my brother
Who said we were friends
In our innocence
We knew that chosen paths have consequences
We became soldiers early
Dressed up in uniforms of wanting more
We fought together in life's battlefield trenches
Long talks, sometime all night
Until the morning sun lends her light
Sometimes sitting talking forever on the veranda
With Ronald and "Brother"
They were our protectors like imaginary fences
Whenever my thoughts take me back to those early days
Courage and destiny take over in so many ways
Frolicking daily in the summertime on the beach
We watched WWF wrestling on tv
After an earlier supper of bread & cheese
Each morning old man Woods would walk in like clockwork
To reveals Glen's future in his everyday speech

Soon after
We moved into this "on your own" world
We face our circumstances, we lost some battles
But we never lost control or sold our souls
Our victories came slowly but they felt so sweet
We came out of an island culture
So we grew accustomed, conditioned to life's heat
Courage is our mantra

We laughed in the face of defeat
Our failures groomed us to do better every day
Our resilience made them old served lemons
packed up and ran away.
For they were dried up, washed up, and lost their taste anyway
We live our lives beyond our regrets
There is no malice in our hearts
If I authored a story about our childhood memories
I would not know where to start
I said it already, and I will say it again with no false pretense
Eternal love my brother
Who said we were friends

Parolee

Bomba Red Reynolds just came home
His skin is polished and his pecs are toned
There is not a single pimple in his face
And dreadlocks falling to his waist
He drinks no liquor he shuns the swine
Have left all that G-life living behind
Bongo-Nya, he uses no brushes, or combs
As sober as ever he feels atoned
Lockdown for fronting powder, guns, and haze
He learnt
a fool and his hustle will soon part ways
Paroled, hardworking, and feeling free
Small footsteps
For it is a long walk back to acceptability
He fights and he struggles to keep above
Seeking help from his homies
but he gets no love
For they are all dead, on lock down, or off on drugs
Evil comes in to spoil the fun
The life of an ex-con just began
His life is a battle that must be won

Survival (the need to win)

Polo Blackmore was always a bully
A glizzy in his waistline, sunglasses covered by a black hoodie
He brought the neighborhood havoc with his gun
But had the other neighborhood "stupids" on the run
Yo Pets! Get ready, it's P B, here he comes
If you do not give it , he takes it
Especially on those days when he pursues his income
He became an eye sore, a leech, a feen, a burden
Something must be done and that's for certain
One Saturday morning early in the A M
Up on third across from Dinos, we all heard the mayhem
That is where the big payback, the gunplay, the karma came in
Not even awaiting angels or prayer could save him
Please hush! We all know he was not a victim
He had many issues mostly with drugs
And the need to win at everything
Born into a broken system
Coupled with those who raised him
This is the final hour, the truth, starts speaking
The block is numb, it has lost all its feelings
He now lay on the cold concrete slowly dying
His help came in slow motion
No rush, no compassion, no one is trying
No one is worried, no one is sorry, no one is crying

Heart of Stone

Who shall come to save us?
I am hurting, for who need times like these
I am frightened and I am nervous
I am asking for all the fighting and the warring to cease
Send home the soldiers for their children are wanting
Daddy's attention is needed
Send him back to us, we want to be fathered in peace
I watched a politician speaking on a global issue today
His speech was cold and long just like winter
He became frozen on what honestly to say
I prayed, that he would just disappear
Pack up his belongings, resign and go away
Just like the last hour of an old year
If you leave now, there will be celebrations everywhere
Haven't we been through enough
All his so-called solutions could easily be rebuffed
Lying in the people's face
Leaving them feeling literally handcuffed
All we are asking
Pack up your belongings, resign and go away
Just like the last hour of an old year
If you leave now, there will be celebrations everywhere
Haven't we been through enough
All your so-called solutions could easily be rebuffed
Stop lying in the people's face
Leaving them with a taste of disgust

Up There (a dope's tale)

Do you want to keep it copacetic?
Let me take you on a ride
I am that home-cooked potent magic
I will have you considering ways to lie
I will take you to the heights of euphoria
Way up there in the sky
Whatever you seek that I will be
You do not have to come down to reality
I promise I will never leave you alone
I will lift you high into the heavens
Into that happy zone
Just fly and fly
Relax, close your eyes, enjoy the ride
You will laugh 'til you cry
You will be singing nursery rhymes to lullabies
I will be your lifetime friend if you have me
For I am that magic flavor
I will keep you buried in the fantasy
I will joyride your life each day
I will keep you climbing, while numbing your pain away
I Just want to fly you like a kite
Don't you worry Liz
You will feel like you are in La La land tonight
And when you drift in and out, or float from high to low
Don't you worry, bro
I will be your winter, keeping you frozen in the snow
Don't you ever feel contrite
You will be gliding in the heavens, morning, noon, and night
I will keep you nice and smooth
Like Coltrane's horn
Or Heather's scrumptious "mac and cheese" on a Sunday afternoon
I will have you flying high and free
Oh no!
There goes my hustle, the "youngin" overdosed on me

The City That Never Sleeps (the failed robbery)

I live in that city that never sleeps
Surrounded by whippersnappers
Criminals, and neighborhood creeps
If they prey on us, It will not come cheap
These Bozos ain't hood, they are from across the street
They came in the back door, masked, with greed and guns
Straight to the safe to steal our funds
Bringing a robbery scheme, these low-down bums
This is when their misery began
They knew it would be crazy, it will be at a cost
These stupids should know better
You do not want smoke with a boss
They came in to score, oh what a loss
I thank you Boogie-down for not raising a fool
Graduated with honors from fight-back School
And so, I reached under the pillow where I kept an extra tool
Where I kept the "just in case money"
Along with pictures of my family jewels
In the darkness I could hear them fuss'
To be honest, their amateur behavior gave me a rush
That is when artillery began to bust
Dreadful things are happening, but not to us
Sparks are flying from beneath the sheets
Mofo's heavy breathing things look bleak
One of the bitch-asses began to speak
Shouting that there is re-enforcement sitting out in the Jeep
So, I separated him from his crew
The hombre kept moving, so I hit him with two
Stupid little "simp" fellow! You know how we do
Block him from involving his peeps

I am lit, got the loser's head spinning
panic is taking over but I will not be sorry for the goons
One by one I blast the stupids'
and still made it to Lauderdale, on Delta, later that afternoon

The Judgement Hour

When tomorrow comes how will I be judged?
Would I be wrapped up in anger?
Or caught up in a blaming game using an aging grudge
Would I be out late at night seeking a buzz?
Wasted in a corner strong-out on regrets, alcohol or drugs
Would my ancestors smile and be proud?
Or would their voices of disappointment silently be loud?
Would my relationship with my siblings and my seed?
Give us time to breathe and heal
Or give the awaiting vultures an opening to fly in to feed
Would the love of family still be embedded in my soul?
Or would I be walking around aimlessly living in my own world?
Would my contemporaries welcome me with open arms?
Or would they be Judases, greet me with a kiss, or pour evil on their
greasy palms?
Would my relationship with the women in my pass?
Comes back to bite me on the ass
Would my earthly friends come in to listen and to stay?
Or would they be deafened, heartless, packed up and run away!
Would my memory of true happiness begin to fade?
Would I have failed to make the grade?
Would the haters write in to throw me shade?
Would they be proxies of a malicious campaign?
Whatever comes I will face because I will never be afraid?
Irene Edna told me to be brave
Your blessings are your jewels, Insha Allah
They would be with you always, from cradle to grave

Master Plan

They say… "what don't kill them fatten"
We are from the house of the forgotten
We fight and so we survive
They came in to redirect our lives
Hoping we will fall off
do hard time for fabricated crimes
Or go in for the suicide, killed by the "popo?, Heck no!
And leave all this good living behind?
There is wisdom in our poverty
You would never hold the power or control over my destiny
So cry for them don't you cry for me
For every man was once a baby

If I were you, I'll fall back
It don't matter if you are a big fish, you know an aristocrat
Our army, God's army is ready to attack
We hope and pray that tomorrow brings
An end to the poor people's suffering
Or else we'll come in and do our thing
It won't be pretty, it could get crazy, for we came to win
Remember in every man's chest a heart beats within
You want to claim we are at peace
We have been down this road before
Seen so many fakes like fleas
Your change of heart we just do not believe
It is in your ammo to lie and cheat
So cry for he who cometh not for he who leaves
So bring your dreams to reality, achieve, achieve!

The Struggle

Tough times move on over
Good times are coming through
Our time is now, we fought the fight
We did the work
We've got this great life of ours to pursue
We are winning at everything, but this we always knew
We live the life we love and love the life we live
We shall only prosper
When we jumped high over those hurdles we learnt how to forgive
The haters are losing, so they complain, treating us like the privileged
We now laugh and laugh deep within
We did not ask, but we were placed in the hard knock's life trenches
We have learnt how to be triumphant
While sitting in deep thoughts into the dark, on them park benches
What we have fought for yesterday, we live it today
But our memories are forever, they will not go away
Way up on this mountainside there stood this sign
It would bring me to thoughts every time
It read "life's path is crazy, that how it is designed"
In life's race some shall walk the journey
And some would be distracted and in so doing shall fall way behind

<u>Crazy Isn't It</u>

It's a crazy world that we are living in
Where everyone hates everything
I took a long walk outside today
I walked and walked, until walking walked away
Nothing seems to have meaning
When joy and happiness began weeping
And truth and government resort to lying
As I walked, I became more confused
Maybe I am walking off my thoughts and views
Maybe I am walking away from the sadness of the daily news
Maybe I am walking to be healthy and buff
Or maybe I've just had enough
Crazy isn't it?

I Cry

I cry for the blessings that brought me here
I cry for family encouragement
They stood there like columns protecting me year after year
I cry not for things that have gone so wrong
I cry for things that have made me strong
I cry for the goodwill people who came along
I cry for the many shoulders that I stand upon
I cry not for life's failures and sadness's
I cry for the unforgettable moments of fun
I cry for the friendships that came and stayed
Not for the hypocrites with their fake-ass praise
Or those who came in just for the motorcade
And through it all I cry for the difference that I have made, if any

Surrounded by Love

My life is surrounded by love
Kissed by the moon, and the heavens above
Each and everyday
Blessings comes my way
And so there I stood having no fear
'Cause all goodwill people came in, just to hear
Stories of my journey
Stories of my life
Lessons on how to survive

O father dear
As a son
A mother's love nothing could compare
I wish they both were here
Your smiles would have been enough
To comfort me when things were tuff
To bring me through those difficult years
I smiled as I fought back the tears
And so each and everyday
Divine blessings came in to say
These are the stories of his journey
These are the stories of his life
These are lessons of how he survived

Happiness has taken control
In my life, in my world
I walked this journey until my feet are bare
I smile to see family, they are soldiers
still fighting, still surviving
Still standing there

Love Ballad

O love, O' ex-woman of mine
From that summer we crossed paths
I knew our lives would be forever intertwined
We tried
I guess our love grew impatiently of being unsatisfied
We cried
We did everything that was possible to keep it going
But intentions and situations cannot hide
Maybe our love was just a season, just passing through
Was the hurt and the frustration all me? Or some were you?
It's brought a familiar flaw that I had, but you already knew
Maybe in another space or phase
Love would have taken us to a forever place
There is this reoccurring conversation that I have with myself
Asking, had I chased her off to live a lie, to love someone else
Maybe our love took us to a false destination
Lost on a journey, walking aimlessly in the wrong direction
They say in due season, everything with meaning, finds redemption
That is our situation, could that be?
Well I guess we will never know… "c'est la vie"!

Heartless

Here comes the freedom that you been fighting for
They say this is the peaceful living that you wanted
Cease fire! There will be no more war
We sent home our soldiers
Their weapons of destruction sit afar
But someone is lying
I could still hear the mother's voices and they were crying
Because their children are still dying
The truth is, you have gotten smarter
Your soldiers no longer wear uniforms
But we will take your nonsense no longer
We have lost our innocence; our silence has all gone
We are the new soldiers
We are dressed up in life-experiences uniforms
We know the fight is not over, we must carry on
We live to fight and fight to win
We will never be concerned about what the setbacks brings
We have this fire, it burns deep within
We shall fight and win over your evil
For truth and goodwill, wins at everything

Drift Like a Memory

All it takes is another love song
To drift us into yesterday's memories
Of love we have lost
And understandings we have gained
We would have fallen hard on the wayside
If we looked for a scapegoat of which to blame
Real love comes at you with no regrets
She holds no dignity, no conditions to restrain
She stands there in our subconscious
She bares no reason to explain

All it takes is another slow song
To remind us of how fragile we are
The need to be right have driven us to squabbles
Then propelled us into a gender war
Treat love like you are a driftwood, floating on the sea
Let her be triumphant
For you would be rewarded, eventually

Benediction

They want to have him crying
Crying in his sleep
For this is their evil wish
That they beg for him this week
He laughed in their faces
For they could not break his soul
He is living his life so peacefully
Just not in their acidic world
He prayed for forgiveness
For wrongs he had done
Then his blessings came in abundance
Evilness is not moving, for her burden weights a ton

A Chaotic World

I sat in prayer with doubt and silence
Watching our lives and our world, losing control
Gobbled up by despair, suffering and violence
Where have our good times basking in the sun have gone
Do we still have energies to fight and to carry on
How many victories shall the heathens hold over us
How could we survive if our lives brings no purpose
Who should we blame? What is its' name? I am so ashamed
For our lives have become a circus
Clowns and puppets shall have no place
If evil or good no longer needs to show its' face
Civility and freedom runs off to space
We become unable to run in a humane race
We journey into an existence in sheer disgrace
We live our lives without purpose, we become displaced
Our survival is losing, and it's at our choosing

Youthfulness

The youthfulness in me is not genetic
It is my capacity to rise above pain and hurt and agony
Letting go of disappointments, loss and regrets
Seeking a better way or bury my thoughts in journeys so faraway
Then looking forward to another tomorrow to bring me a better day
With laughter, great family and real friendships at my side
I found and flushed out, bitterness and sourness from my mind
Telling myself that tomorrow shall restore all my joy and all my
happiness
Then blessings and goodwill shall come in to do the rest
I have never worried about things I cannot change
And negative energies and burdens have drifted off beyond my reach
for their chaotic taste, has no place
I live life to be a better person everyday
I watch stress and misery, who loves company,
Gets pissed and fed-up, get up and walk away
Tomorrow means expectancy
For I have no idea what she has in store for me
But whatever she brings it would be embraced in my world
My youthfulness comes from laughter, prayer and an emancipated
soul

The Golden Years

Believe me!
A lot is on my mind, for moving away does not come easily
The time is getting closer and closer for me to flee this city
I am getting too old for the same old routine
Those so-called city leaders, they have failed
Makes me want to intervene
The everyday frustrations travelling the cages back and forth
To work the nine to five
I am trying, but I am fading deep down inside
It is too cold! In seconds dreadful things could unfold
Crime has gotten out of control! I need a new purpose in my world
I am all into the second cycle of my copasetic life
I am forever skirt chasing, but I would rather settle down with a wife
I am going to a place where the sun shines a little longer and much
stronger
And if it gets cold
All I would need is two shots of ripple, and a St. John's Bay Cotton
sweater
Wherever I shall be
My family will still be around me, so it does not matter
I am off to a place much slower to start my second chapter
Friends in my life they would know how to find me
To keep it a buck, man friendships I do not have many
A minute of silence to those who fought in the trenches that I have
lost
A trip to Alkebulan, my ancestral land, who cares what it cost
Woman in my life if she stays true I probably wife it
She flips on me, then she should buy a dog, die alone, go marry your
bullshit
Awaiting those long walks on the beach

Playing dominoes daily I have become one of those Old-timers across the street
Look at me, shirtless, with an aging physique, taking in the heat
Sipping' on some homemade lemonade, while sitting on a bench looking out at the ocean
Man! This is living
I love my newfound situation
I shall live the rest of my life, living my life in a celebration

Waiting In Vain

It is so evident that I am only counting the "wins"
I have regrouped, I have fixed, cast off the bricks
Then purposed into my future the better of things
So many years, too many years, I have spent second-guessing
Living in the shadows, living my life on the decline
Fortunately, those tapes cannot be recovered or await a rewind
Selah! I am more seasoned and much older now
I was granted the formula to win, somewhere, somehow
I now look at life, my life in a remarkable way
Today brings tomorrow, in my world there is no yesterday
Great experiences and resolve I have gained
Journeys of joy or sorrow, sunshine or rain
I have watered with laughter my garden of pain
Which has reaped fruits of happiness
My orchard of purpose has been reclaimed
The loss of time, is never regained
The weight of wasted time, is to be waiting in vain

Aging

Oh wow, I am getting much older
Faces and colors begins to fade
Look how I am getting slower and slower by the hour
Especially when I am walking up those stairs
I still hear familiar voices
But they get more distant year after year
I am still an early riser
I am outside walking and observing everything near the pier
I am cautious but not fearful
For there are cameras and cellphones everywhere

I reminisce about the wars that I have fought
And celebrate the battles that I have won
For me, the 9-5 is over
And my golden years has now begun
I still greet the new day each morning
I still find ways to earn my fun
The depressing cable morning news
leaves me numb and so confused
But it will never steal my fun
Winter snow is melting
So, I await the springtime bird's songs to come
Another April's Birthday has come and gone
Then here comes the summer's sun
I have drained all my tears
I have lived beyond all my fears
I sit on the park's bench much longer now
Watching how time "tick-tocks" and disappears

Return to Dust

Fly away son!, fly on!, fly on!
Please do not cry for me
Now that I am gone
Lay me to rest under the shade of a sycamore tree
Let the rain, the sun, the wind
And all the other elements that are earthly
Take hold of me for my flesh is of them
Let the seeds of my parents and the seed of mine
Bring me flowers and berries
Mangoes, and cherries
Created from the blossoms of yesterday
I need that sweet smell of nectar to be everlasting
My soul is sailing on this journey home
It is a journey I must take alone
Going, going, gone, fly on, fly on
For it is now my turn
The life I have lived is the life I have earned
I have been so lucky for love has never left me
Look at the love you have come here today to share
Stay true, speak of the life I have lived
Play me songs of yesterday that I love, I'll smile into its rhythm
Have them tell a story, yes my life's journey
Play me audio sounds of the waves from the Carib's Sea
Then read me verses of freedom from the books of Maccabee
Have my head rest, so mine eyes sees the rising sun
Remember shed no tears for me please
For I am free, free of Babylon
Don't you dare utter a sadden speech
For only deaf ears your utterance shall reach
Give a minute of silence
So we could all listen and enjoy the peace
Could you hear the tides from the distant beach?
Here comes that Nichola Town breeze
Then play me some sweet music
Yes, play me that sweet freedom music, "you dig" ...good!
And now let us pray for the street people
The forgotten, the downtrodden, those at the bottom
From the house of Timbuktu, to the city of Gotham
They fight each day to survive
Your view of them is so wrong

But they will not give up, they will stay strong
And to be honest, I was one of them all along
So please don't you cry for me
I say, see you later for this is what life wrote for me
I am free, I am free
See you in paradise
Remember my love, is a river of love, which shall flow eternally
Look! look around you...that's me, that's me
See you in paradise...love eternally

www.ingramcontent.com/pod-product-compliance
Lightning Source LLC
Chambersburg PA
CBHW070747280626
47162CB00017B/2467